THE
LEARNING NEEDS ANALYSIS
POCKETBOOK

By Paul Donovan and John Townsend

Drawings by Phil Hailstone

"Concise yet comprehensive, a handy and valuable resource for training professionals."
Justin Kinnear, Education & Training Manager, IBM Sales & Marketing Centre EMEA

"Paul and John have once again provided a really practical set of tools in a well-structured and accessible format. The six windows will certainly help readers focus quickly on what matters."
David Backhouse, Head of Learning & Development, Thames Valley Police

"Accurate, precise, thorough and an invaluable tool for anyone involved in identifying training and development needs."
Brian Kirwan, Human Resources Director, Irish Blood Transfusion Service

Published by:
Management Pocketbooks Ltd
Laurel House, Station Approach, Alresford, Hants SO24 9JH, U.K.
Tel: +44 (0)1962 735573   Fax: +44 (0)1962 733637
E-mail: sales@pocketbook.co.uk
Website: www.pocketbook.co.uk

© Paul Donovan and John Townsend 2004, 2015

First published 2004 as Training Needs Analysis Pocketbook
ISBN 978 1 903776 24 7

This edition published 2015. ISBN 978 1 906610 71 5

E-book ISBN 978 1 908284 37 2

British Library Cataloguing-in-Publication Data – A catalogue record for this book is available from the British Library.

Design, typesetting and graphics by **efex ltd**. Printed in U.K.

CONTENTS

PREFACE

Since the first edition of this pocketbook appeared in 2004, the focus of training has changed. Organisations are looking more and more at their employees' immediate learning needs rather than conducting systematic and sometimes laborious analyses of their training needs, and the emphasis is shifting away from providing a catalogue of training opportunities to organising 'just-in-time' learning to cope with business/environmental changes.

On top of this, organisations and managers are increasingly uncertain about the value they get in return for their investment in training. In 2012, the American Society for Training and Development (now renamed as ATD, the Association for Talent Development) estimated that organisations invest $156bn annually on training. Many consider that a lot of this investment is wasted because, after just one year, employees retain only 10% to 15% of what they have learned.

This is why we've streamlined the pocketbook. The title has been changed to **Learning Needs Analysis** and we've outlined a new 'cut-to-the-chase' approach to investigating learning needs – the **Six Windows**.

John & Paul 2014

INTRODUCTION

DEFINITION

Learning needs analysis is identifying the new knowledge, skills and attitudes which people require to meet their own and their organisation's development needs.

PURPOSE & FORMAT

The purpose of this pocketbook is to simplify learning needs analysis.
You may have the impression that LNA (as we'll abbreviate it in the book), is a rather boring, time-consuming and somewhat bureaucratic process. We hope to show you that it can be strategic, rewarding, career-enhancing and even...fun!

To simplify things even more, we've divided the book into three main sections:

- **The Six Windows** – an easy-to-follow needs identification checklist that will help you go straight to the **source** of your organisation's employee learning needs

- **The Ten Point Training Plan** – the document, spreadsheet or wall chart where you can record all your notes from your learning needs investigation and plan for each training course or event

- **The Tool Box** – crammed full of instruments, methods, tips and techniques to help you do a great job at every step of the LNA process

STORY

Once upon a time a competent young training manager of a fairly large manufacturing company was asked to do a professional analysis of the training needs of all the organisation's 5000 employees. What a great job she did!

Skills matrices were completed for all the operators and checked with each of them for accuracy, as well as in-depth interviews to analyse competency gaps for the office staff and the managers. Armed with an ocean of data, her department designed and organised the delivery of a series of top-class training courses – each one created with behaviourally stated learning objectives to help participants close their competency/skills, knowledge and attitude gaps.

The end-of-course evaluation sheets completed by every participant showed unanimous satisfaction with an average overall score of four out of five.

However, three months after the training courses had all been completed, the president of the firm called the training manager to his office and told her that company results were **worse** than they had been before the training!

WHAT WENT WRONG?

Following an investigation into what went wrong the young training manager was able to establish:

- Insufficient connection between the training design and the mission of the organisation. The mission wasn't clearly defined so the training that was delivered missed the mark

- A lack of focus on the business goals and objectives that training could have supported

- The existing culture was resistant to the changes being put forward in the training, eg people were **rewarded** for rapid output while being **trained** to slow down and improve quality

- The organisation's structures and processes did not support the training messages (eg 14 layers of hierarchy existed while the training emphasised the empowerment of staff)

- The technology needed to implement the new skills was not available back on the job

- The company compensation system rewarded individual effort whereas the training concentrated on teamwork

INTRODUCTION

RESEARCH & OBSERVATION

As we mention in the preface, our research and observation in the area of LNA points to an alarmingly high level of wastage when it comes to the retention and transfer of learning from training. Some research* has suggested that as much as 90% of the learning is never applied back on the job. In our experience, most of this wastage occurs for one of three reasons:

1. Like the story on page 8, the training is not transferred to the job either for **cultural reasons** (no interest or reward from the organisation for people to change their behaviour and apply the learning) or for **structural reasons** (barriers to new skills or lack of opportunity to use them). See also page 94.

2. Training design and/ or delivery is poor and therefore not seen as useful or relevant.

3. The participants are not willing, able or 'needy' to learn.

* So Much Training, So Little to Show for It, Rachel Emma Silverman,
Wall Street Journal Oct. 26, 2012.

STAKEHOLDERS – WHAT'S THEIR ROLE?

SENIOR MANAGEMENT	To tell us what their goals are so we know what to concentrate on.
LINE MANAGEMENT	To help us turn the organisation's goals into performance requirements and learning objectives, and to identify gaps in team and individual performance.
TRAINING DEPARTMENT	To develop a training and development policy for the organisation, to drive a learning needs assessment and to turn learning objectives into learning opportunities.
JOB HOLDERS	To identify gaps in their own performance and to help in the search to close them.

INTRODUCTION

CUT TO THE CHASE

To avoid the pitfalls of a lot of 'traditional' training needs analysis approaches, and the dangers of failed training (see example on pages 8 and 9), you, the HRD professionals in today's fast moving and ruthlessly lean economic environment, need to ask the following questions:

1. What business is our organisation in? How is it different from other enterprises?

2. What is our organisation's strategy? How does it plan to reach its goals?

3. What internal organisational issues have to be considered on a regular basis – culture, size, stability, etc?

4. Who are its people? What are the organisation's demographics, skills, diversities, etc?

Once you have this clear **overall** picture of your organisation, the next chapter will provide you with six windows – six ways of looking into the organisation – with a view to identifying the pressing and results-oriented learning needs of its most important asset.
Look on….!

THE SIX WINDOWS

THE SIX WINDOWS

LOOK THROUGH ANY WINDOW

Traditional training needs analysis approaches (including our own!) have advocated systematic and relatively labour intensive investigations. Academics have proposed looking at different levels of needs (ie organisational, group and individual).

Our observations of how organisations are actually working these days show that there are six fundamental areas where employees' learning needs are being identified and assessed rapidly and efficiently. We suggest that you can look through any or all of these 'windows' to see what learning needs are there – right in front of your eyes or out on the horizon:

- Compliance needs (organisation, industry or nation-wide)
- Human resource planning
- Succession planning
- Critical incidents
- Management information systems
- Performance appraisal

WINDOW 1. COMPLIANCE NEEDS

DEFINITION

Most of the learning needs that we identify may be described as discretionary, in that the organisation has some choice whether or not to implement. Take, for example, leadership training for senior managers. If the organisation chooses not to implement this training its success may suffer long-term because of missed opportunities. However, it's highly unlikely that it will go bankrupt in the short-term solely because this training was not available.

Compliance training is usually not discretionary. It is imposed, generally by outside regulatory agencies, including the Government, to ensure that certain standards of performance are achieved by all market players, but sometimes by an organisation's corporate headquarters in order to roll out subsidiary-wide performance standards.

WINDOW 1. COMPLIANCE NEEDS

INTERNAL COMPLIANCE

Internal compliance refers to training related to an organisation's mission/ strategy which is 'rolled out' to all employees – sometimes referred to as wall-to-wall training. Examples of this include:

- **Orientation:** often offered for all employees to ensure awareness of and adherence to organisational and cultural requirements

- **Customer service:** companies, such as ASDA Retail and Marks and Spencer, ensure that staff training prioritises this critical area

- **New product:** training for all staff in the benefits and features of company innovations

- **Mergers/ acquisitions:** provided when employees need assistance to cope with the stresses and opportunities involved in takeovers

WINDOW 1. COMPLIANCE NEEDS

EXTERNAL COMPLIANCE

External compliance refers to training imposed by the requirements of an external agency, such as legal requirements of the State. Examples include:

- **Health and Safety:** construction firms having to train employees in safety measures before they set foot on site
- **Diversity:** organisations needing to train managers in their legal obligations in the area of equal opportunities
- **Bullying/ harassment:** managers being made aware of their responsibility to protect employees against attacks on their dignity
- **Ethics training:** financial services firms requiring their employees to participate in ethics training to ensure appropriate treatment of customers
- **Quality procedures:** pharmaceutical firms training and retraining employees in order to comply with external regulations (eg FDA requirements)

THE SIX WINDOWS

WINDOW 1. COMPLIANCE NEEDS
WHO TO ASK

This kind of training will differ from firm to firm and may be confusing for the newly appointed HRD executive. It can be a good idea to have face-to-face conversations with senior executives, such as the organisation's legal advisor, the Chief Financial Officer, or the Operations Director.

These people have responsibilities to ensure that their firm does not fall foul of the externally and internally mandated requirements. As always in training, your job is to help them do their job!

WINDOW 2. HUMAN RESOURCE PLANNING

DEFINITION

Human resource planning is about putting the right people in the right place at the right time. As with many succinct HR concepts, it's easy to describe but not quite so simple to put into practice, given the incredible speed of change in organisations these days.

HR planning has a very big impact on training. As the need for different types and/ or different numbers of staff change, there is an immediate impact on the learning needs of present and future employees.

This is the case whether employee numbers are increasing **or** decreasing.

WINDOW 2. HUMAN RESOURCE PLANNING

EXAMPLE

Here's an example of the impact of HR planning on learning needs:

By the end of 2012 the total number of employees in Ireland's public sector was approximately 291,000 – 30% lower than in 2008. So…fewer people to train? In fact, there's probably **more** training to be done! Why?

Because of the increased demand for services such as education and health provision, employees are being redeployed and managers are having to do more work with fewer people.

Retirements and attrition among supervisors mean that bosses are often responsible for even greater numbers of people, and they need new managerial skills.

So, contrary to first impressions, there has been an **increase** in their learning needs!

WINDOW 2. HUMAN RESOURCE PLANNING

EXAMPLE

When an organisation is expanding it's much clearer that learning needs will also be growing. However, it's easy to underestimate the numbers required. For example, let's say you work in HRD for an internet consumer to consumer company and they want to open a call centre catering solely for the Chinese market. Here's an estimate of the number of call agents you'll need each year for the next five years:

 1000 1250 1500 1750 2000

A simple calculation shows that you will need to train 250 call agents per year to keep up with demand. But, if you did that you'd fall considerably short of the actual headcount need.

Why? First, you have to factor in labour turnover. At just 10% you would still need an extra 100 recruits trained in the first year. Also, some employees won't succeed in the training exams and will lose their jobs. Even if this failure rate was as low as 2% you'd still be looking for an extra 20 recruits to train in the first year.

21

WINDOW 3. SUCCESSION PLANNING
SUCCESS & SUCCESSION

When Sir Alex Ferguson retired as manager of Manchester United Football Club, fans all over the world were talking about succession planning. Who would succeed him? When Apple's Steve Jobs died in 2011 there was a lot of speculation about his replacement. Since most organisations these days can't just go out to the market and buy a ready-made replacement in the way operations like Manchester United can, it's vital to have an internal source of replacement. You also need a training plan to meet the promoted star's learning needs to bring them to high performance as soon as possible.

THE SIX WINDOWS

WINDOW 3. SUCCESSION PLANNING

ORGANISATION CHART

To look through the succession planning window, HRD practitioners should keep a copy of the organisation chart to hand as an 'early warning' planning tool for identifying the learning needs of certain employees. The organisation chart obviously doesn't **specifically** highlight learning needs, but, if properly used, it can be one of your best sources. How long before Ms. X retires? Who's next in line if Mr. Y is headhunted away? What if….?

Example with incumbent's age and number of years to retirement

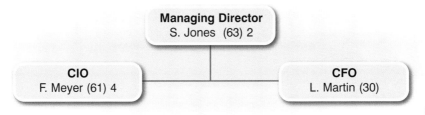

WINDOW 3. SUCCESSION PLANNING
EXAMPLE

The organisation chart on the previous page shows us that Jones, the Managing Director, is going to retire in two years' time. It's likely that Meyer, if appointed, will simply be a 'stop-gap' replacement – having only two further years to retirement himself. Martin could then be a possible replacement if, over the next four years, she can acquire the necessary competencies to perform the role.

This is a decision for senior management but your job as an HRD professional would be to assess what Martin needs to learn in preparation for the role and make a proposal. Given that the search for an executive usually costs about 25% of the person's annual salary, the training you propose could help save the organisation a lot of money. Of course, you will also be looking to see who could take over from Meyer and Martin in their current roles, either internally or externally. If there's someone in the organisation already, what are their learning needs?

WINDOW 4. CRITICAL INCIDENTS

DEFINITION

Critical incidents are sudden and negative departures from expected business performance, usually due to a relatively dramatic event or to a change in group or individual behaviour. Often one leads to the other. The word *incident* reflects that it's either one single event or a series of events within a short time frame.

When a critical incident occurs, such as a fire in a factory or a sudden decrease in performance of the sales team in a service organisation, we'll often hear calls for extra training to be provided to deal with the problem.

WINDOW 4. CRITICAL INCIDENTS

ANALYSING INCIDENTS: THE FIVE QUESTIONS

Imagine that you work for a large telecom carrier and that the performance of the sales team has suddenly dropped significantly. This is a critical incident. In a situation like this management might panic and call for immediate remedial training. Keep calm! Before spending precious resources on training you need to find out whether learning needs really lie at the heart of the problem. To do this you need to answer five questions:

1. **What exactly is the problem?** How big is the drop in sales? What level of sales is acceptable given present circumstances…what's the size of the problem?

2. **When did the problem happen?** The answer might coincide with a change in policy/ procedure or the introduction of new software, which in turn will point to a very specific learning need to be met with a fast training solution.

WINDOW 4. CRITICAL INCIDENTS

ANALYSING INCIDENTS: THE FIVE QUESTIONS

3. **Where is the problem taking place (and where not?)** Is the problem company-wide, only in the domestic operations or overseas or mainly in one office? Again the answer will pinpoint possible learning needs (or something else entirely!).

4. **Who is the problem happening with?** Is the problem only with new entrants, or among experienced sales staff? If, for example, it's occurring with inductees from a recent orientation programme only, then there's probably something going wrong with that training.

5. **Why is it happening?** This should now be obvious from the answers to the other four questions.

We then move forward armed with the information and the knowledge that if we do decide to implement a learning initiative, it will be for the right reasons. It will take strong nerves to resist the pressure from management to provide instant training if, in fact, the problem does **not** stem from learning needs.

WINDOW 5. MANAGEMENT INFORMATION SYSTEMS

A SOURCE OF LEARNING NEEDS?

Management Information Systems present up-to-date real-time information to the organisation's leaders on what's actually going on. HRD professionals should always try to be present at the regular meetings where this data is discussed.

Looking in through the MIS window gives you a clear picture of the organisation's *here and now*. The latest figures/ findings/ results are the life blood of change and being there when the 'live' data is presented means that you can immediately suggest useful training interventions.

THE SIX WINDOWS

WINDOW 5. MANAGEMENT INFORMATION SYSTEMS

EXAMPLES OF DATA TO ANALYSE

Many of the facts and figures that are the foundations on which management decisions are built can also be strong indicators of learning needs. The kinds of data you should be monitoring include:

- **Sales data by department/ product line, etc** – are new skills or knowledge needed?
- **Waste and quality figures** – are standards slipping? Do people need new skills or top-up training?
- **Accident and other safety figures** – maybe compliance re-training is required
- **Staff turnover statistics** – an increase may be caused by employee dissatisfaction and could point to a learning need for supervisors in leadership and motivation
- **Customer complaints** – if they are increasing do we need new or catch-up customer service training?

WINDOW 6. PERFORMANCE APPRAISAL

PLUGGING THE GAPS

Most organisations today have a relatively formal, usually top down, approach to performance appraisal where line managers assess an employee's performance over a certain period of time and, in a performance review meeting, agree on a plan for how they can improve.

Performance management should be an ongoing process where managers regularly appraise, guide, coach and encourage better performance levels from their staff. The information from appraisals will indicate specific performance gaps and help to identify the 'real time' learning needs that have been agreed between the manager and employee (see also pages 71-74).

THE TEN POINT TRAINING PLAN

THE TEN POINT TRAINING PLAN

DESCRIPTION

The **ten point training plan** is a document that will help you to record the results of your learning needs analysis and how you intend to put into practice the learning objectives you identified.

The plan could take the form of a report, a spreadsheet or even a wall chart.

In total the ten elements of a good training plan are:

1 Vision/mission/strategy

2 Performance issue being addressed

3 Specific learning objectives

4 Participant categories

5 Methods of participant selection

6 Outline of training solution (course(s))

7 Who will deliver the training?

8 Training delivery standards

9 Roles and responsibilities

10 Evaluation criteria

THE TEN POINT TRAINING PLAN

WHAT TO INCLUDE

 VISION/ MISSION/ STRATEGY

Assuming that your organisation has a published vision/mission/strategy statement you need first to find an extract from it which endorses, justifies and validates the need for the kind of training you are planning to develop, and then include it at the beginning of your ten point plan.

If your organisation does not have a written vision, mission and strategy then it's useful to try to elicit what they are – they do exist, you know! You can find out by asking a few questions and by seeking some documents that should be available within your organisation.

The organisation's **vision** can be identified by interviewing the CEO and by trying to find out how he/she **sees** the firm now and into the future. What is their **picture** of the firm? Ask them to describe it in vivid terms. If a vision has not been drawn up for your organisation, the answers that you get may well be vague and unspecific. Don't give up. Keep asking, 'Why this?', 'Why that?' Ask your CEO to explain to you what purpose, apart from making money or providing such and such services, the organisation fulfils. The more you persist the more clear it will become.

THE TEN POINT TRAINING PLAN

WHAT TO INCLUDE

1 VISION/ MISSION/ STRATEGY

Establishing an organisation's **mission and strategy** is really about asking five questions. These are:

1. What products and/or services does the organisation provide? What market or public sector is it in?
2. How does it provide those services? In what way does it position itself in this market? What beliefs and values drive the way it conducts its activities?
3. Who does it provide these benefits for? Who are the customers and consumers?
4. Who does it use to provide them? Who are its allies and strategic collaborators including its own suppliers?
5. Why does it supply these benefits? What is its overall purpose?

WHAT TO INCLUDE

PERFORMANCE ISSUE BEING ADDRESSED

One way of making sure that your training solution hits the mark is to remind yourself constantly of the performance issues the training is trying to deal with (see previous chapter). This is, if you will, the 'title' section for each planned course or intervention.

THE TEN POINT TRAINING PLAN

WHAT TO INCLUDE

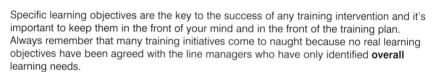

SPECIFIC LEARNING OBJECTIVES

Specific learning objectives are the key to the success of any training intervention and it's important to keep them in the front of your mind and in the front of the training plan. Always remember that many training initiatives come to naught because no real learning objectives have been agreed with the line managers who have only identified **overall** learning needs.

Questions which will help elicit learning objectives from line managers might include:

- What, specifically, will people be able to do differently when the training is over?
- What competencies will they be able to display?
- What will you accept as evidence that the learning has been successful?

To learn how to write **learning objectives** see pages 77-78.
For tips on writing **competencies** see pages 49-53.
Other methods for quantifying learning needs include using **focus groups** – see pages 75-76 – and **stakeholder analysis** – see pages 68-69.

WHAT TO INCLUDE

PARTICIPANT CATEGORIES

This section of your training plan covers the types/ groups of employees who will be targeted for this training. It will also detail categories that may be excluded from the training.

You'll obviously get this information from your learning needs analysis notes.

WHAT TO INCLUDE

5 METHODS OF PARTICIPANT SELECTION

This will be a key and relatively lengthy section of your training plan. In order to choose actual participants from the employee categories targeted, you will need to decide on the 'gap identification tools', which will show you which people are lacking which knowledge, skills or attitudes in terms of the new performance goals.

The reader of your training plan will want to know how you decided on the contents of the training and how/why individual participants will be selected to attend.

In this section, therefore, you should describe the source of the learning needs as well as the gap identification tools you have chosen from pages 55-74 of the Tool Box section of this book (for example: competency audit, interviews, skills matrix, performance appraisal, etc).

WHAT TO INCLUDE

6 OUTLINE OF TRAINING SOLUTION

This section of your plan will be more or less detailed depending on how many training events you are planning. The level of detail may vary from:

- Course title, sub-title and learning objectives

to

- A complete description of each module

THE TEN POINT TRAINING PLAN

WHAT TO INCLUDE

7 WHO WILL DELIVER THE TRAINING?

In this section you should include the names
and CVs of the trainers who will deliver your
courses. The CVs should contain enough
information to justify their selection and
be open to challenge by managers and
participants.

THE TEN POINT TRAINING PLAN

WHAT TO INCLUDE

8 ▶ TRAINING DELIVERY STANDARDS

This part should be a standard element of every training plan, and could even be pre-printed. It represents the organisation's required level of quality concerning:

- Course joining instructions
- Venue management
- Professional training delivery

THE TEN POINT TRAINING PLAN

WHAT TO INCLUDE

9 ROLES & RESPONSIBILITIES

In this section of the training plan it's important to outline the roles and responsibilities of the main triangle of stakeholders involved in training, because training transfer is often spoilt by a failure of one of the parties to fulfil their role:

- **Participant** – prepare personal learning objectives for the course; be present 100% of time; participate enthusiastically; attend pre- and post-course briefings and follow-up meetings with boss and/or trainer

- **Training department** – conduct the learning needs assessment; draw up training plans; administer joining instructions; organise and supervise delivery of training; conduct evaluations and follow-up

- **Manager** – participate in the learning needs assessment; support and brief participants before, during and after the training; set measurable objectives and reward the practice of learning

THE TEN POINT TRAINING PLAN

WHAT TO INCLUDE

 EVALUATION CRITERIA

This last part of the training plan is where you describe the criteria and the process that you have agreed with line management will be used to evaluate the success of the training.

This will ensure that you are protected against 'moving goal posts', revisionism and bad faith following the training event.

It can also help to focus everyone's attention on transfer because when you are clear on what to evaluate it is so much easier to organise for success!

See the Tool Box section on pages 96-97 for a summary of the four levels of training evaluation, or *The Training Evaluation Pocketbook* in this series for more detail on how to measure training success.

FURTHER READING

You are now half way through the LNA pocketbook. Before you look into the specific hands-on tools that follow, here are a few books you might find useful to complement your learning on learning needs analysis!

A Practical Guide to Needs Assessment, Kavita Gupta, John Wiley & Sons, 2011

A Practical Guide to Needs Assessment (2nd ed.), K. Gupta, C. Sleezer & D. Russ-Eft, Pfeiffer, 2007

First Things Fast: A Handbook for Performance Analysis (Essential Knowledge Resource). 2nd ed, A. Rossett, Jossey-Bass, 2009

Needs Assessment Basics, D. Tobey, ASTD Press, 2005

Needs Assessment for Organizational Success. R. Kaufman & I. Guerra-Lopez, ASTD Press, 2013

The Needs Assessment KIT. (ed.), J. W. Altschuld, SAGE Publications, 2010

The Needs Assessment KIT – Book 5 Phase 3: Taking Action for Change, L. Stevahn & J. King, SAGE Publications, 2010

Training Needs Analysis and Evaluation, F. Bee & R. Bee, CIPD, 1997

Training Needs Assessment: Methods, tools and techniques, J. Barbazette, Pfeiffer, 2006

Training Trilogy: Conducting Needs Assessment, Designing Programs, Training Skills, D. Leatherman, Resource Development Press, 2007

TOOL BOX

TOOL BOX

FORCE FIELD ANALYSIS

DEFINITION & METHODOLOGY

Force field analysis (FFA) is a simple method for visualising the things that will help or hinder any proposed change, so that you can plan for **realistic** implementation of your actions. For example, it would be a good tool with which to test the feasibility of performance goals set as a result of training.

How?

- Write the **new performance goal** on the top of a flipchart/pinboard

- Divide the sheet in two: **Help** and **Hinder**

- Brainstorm on Post-its all the things which are 'enablers' and will help people change, and those 'obstacles' which may stand in their way

(See examples on next two pages.)

FORCE FIELD ANALYSIS

EXAMPLE 1

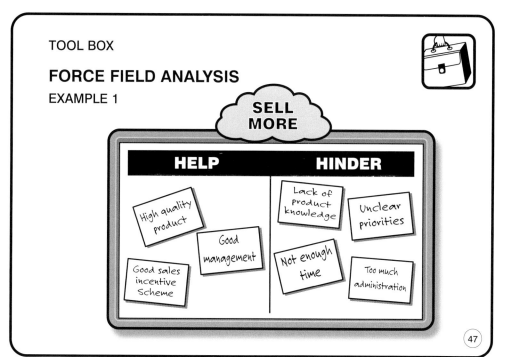

FORCE FIELD ANALYSIS

EXAMPLE 2

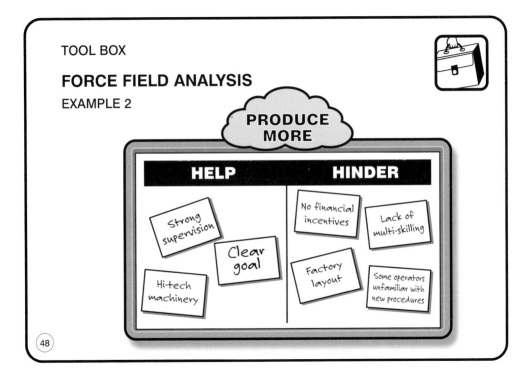

PRODUCE MORE

HELP	HINDER
Strong supervision	No financial incentives
Clear goal	Lack of multi-skilling
Hi-tech machinery	Factory layout
	Some operators unfamiliar with new procedures

COMPETENCIES

DEFINITION

In this section, we're going to show you how to describe, 'dose' (see page 52) and find ways to strengthen competencies before going on to look at how you can measure people's 'gaps'.

To keep it simple we've defined competencies as:

The behaviour patterns, based on acquired knowledge, skills and attitudes, which a person needs to bring to a job in order to carry out certain key tasks with competence.

So, when we define new performance goals we need to elaborate new competencies.

COMPETENCIES
HOW TO DESCRIBE THEM

Once key tasks have been identified for a job, a good competency description will meet the following criteria:

- Behaviourally stated (how people should do things)
- Observable and measurable
- Culturally congruent (should reflect the organisational culture)
- Stand-alone (no overlaps with other competencies)

TOOL BOX

COMPETENCIES

EXAMPLE FOR AIRPORT SECURITY EMPLOYEE

KEY TASK

Checks boarding passes, tickets and permits in order to detect fraud and ensure airline and airport security

COMPETENCY

- Questions passengers and staff courteously but assertively

- Recognises validity of all tickets, boarding passes and other airport permits for travel or access to terminals

MEASURE

- Averages 80% on the checklist of agreed courteous and assertive behaviours made by observer

- 90% accuracy of recognition during spot check by manager

COMPETENCIES
'DOSES' OF COMPETENCE

To 'dose' a competence simply means to describe the various amounts of ability and skills needed to deliver performance in a key task area.

In other words, **describe the kind of knowledge, skills and attitudes demonstrated by people who are:**

Developing this competence
Operational in this competence
Strong in this competence
Excellent in this competence

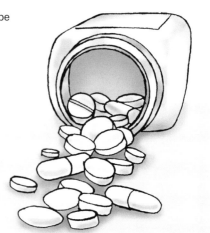

TOOL BOX

COMPETENCIES
'DOSES' OF COMPETENCE

EXAMPLE FOR AIRPORT SECURITY EMPLOYEE

COMPETENCY

Questions passengers and staff courteously but assertively	KEY TASK Checks boarding passes and permits

Developing	Checks documents in a perfunctory manner. Questions people impersonally without warmth or politeness.
Operational	Same as level one but with personal eye contact and politeness.
Strong	Checks documents, asks questions with a smile and addresses people as 'Sir' or 'Madam' (if possible 'Mr or Ms XYZ').
Excellent	Creates a warm 'moment of truth' – ie treats each individual as a special and valued customer. Enquires about their journey and engages in brief, friendly banter.

COMPETENCIES

HOW TO STRENGTHEN THEM

Training may be only one of literally hundreds of ways to help people strengthen their competencies.

We suggest the use of a focus group (see page 75) as one solution. Call together a group of people specialised in the competency in question and brainstorm creative/cost-effective activities which will accelerate the development of the necessary knowledge, skills and attitudes.

TOOL BOX

COMPETENCIES

COMPETENCY AUDIT

A competency audit is a way of identifying the gaps in an individual's competence at performing their key tasks.

As part of LNA, the competency audit will help you find out **who** needs **what** development in the areas which have been highlighted in your analysis.

TOOL BOX

COMPETENCIES

COMPETENCY AUDIT: EXAMPLE 1 – Airport Security Employee

KEY TASK: Checks boarding passes and permits

COMPETENCY	IMPORTANCE TO JOB (1-5)	Developing ? Operational ? Strong ? Excellent ?
Questions passengers and staff courteously but assertively.		
Recognises validity of all tickets, boarding passes and other airport permits.		

TOOL BOX

COMPETENCIES

COMPETENCY AUDIT: EXAMPLE 2 – Team Manager

KEY TASK: Facilitates team meetings

COMPETENCY	IMPORTANCE TO JOB (1-5)	**D**eveloping ? **O**perational ? **S**trong ? **E**xcellent ?
Suggests meeting agenda and processes for problem-solving and decision-making.		
Listens actively by checking understanding and agreement of others.		

IDENTIFYING COMPETENCY GAPS
SKILLS MATRIX (aka VERSATILITY CHARTS)

Skills matrices are means of recording and consolidating the skill levels of any number of team members across a range of skill areas. A skills matrix can be completed using the boss's judgement only or by using a participatory approach with team members.

Legend:
- No Knowledge or Skills
- Basic knowledge
- Some experience
- Competent under supervision
- Fully competent

NAME	Induction completed	Safety training completed	Word Processing	Cash Accounting	Reception	Filing	Inter-personal	E-mail	Action
O'Connor	✓	✓							Word Processing/E-mail course next Autumn
Reilly	✓								Intensive training to catch up with team
Khan	✓	✓							E-mail course next Autumn
Sullivan	✓	✓							E-mail course next Autumn
Donovan	✓								E-mail course next Autumn
Lopez		✓							Word Processing/E-mail course next Autumn

TOOL BOX

IDENTIFYING COMPETENCY GAPS
STRUCTURED INTERVIEWS

There are hundreds of formats for establishing competency gaps at the individual level, using interviews, surveys and questionnaires.

Structured interviews, carried out by the training professional/performance consultant with individuals who have been targeted as needing to meet new performance goals, are time-consuming but rewarding. Rewarding because well-constructed questions can help you ensure that you end up with real training needs based on real, accepted gaps in people's skills and not just 'wants'.

Good interviews also help you avoid conducting 'wall-to-wall carpeting' or 'sheep dip' type training where everyone has to go to a course whether or not they need it. Part of the purported 90% of wasted training comes from teaching people things they already know or that they don't really need for their jobs.

(This kind of training can be justified, though, when the CEO sincerely wants all employees to attend an event as part of a company 'values identification' drive, or when the training is mandatory (see pages 15-18))

IDENTIFYING COMPETENCY GAPS
STRUCTURED INTERVIEWS – EXAMPLE

Opening Question:
'Under the following headings, what training would help you become effective in meeting your new performance goals?'

Technical, job-related training?	
How specifically will this help you?	
Interpersonal skills training?	
How specifically will this help you?	
Information?	
What information do you need and how will it help you exactly?	

IDENTIFYING COMPETENCY GAPS
360° QUESTIONNAIRES

Getting feedback from 'all around' a person (ie from boss, colleagues and subordinates as well as from the individual) can give a much clearer and fairer picture of that individual's development needs than feedback from just a single source.

360° surveys on individuals are expensive and time-consuming and are usually reserved for senior management. However, the relatively low risk aspect of acting only on consensus points means that subsequent training action is tailor-made to the job and to the organisation's needs.

TOOL BOX

IDENTIFYING COMPETENCY GAPS

360° QUESTIONNAIRES – SAMPLE

How does the person you are scoring rate on the following issue?
Please mark an x on the line.
(1 = Low, 5 = High)

1　　　　**2**　　　　**3**　　　　**4**　　　　**5**

IDENTIFYING COMPETENCY GAPS

360° QUESTIONNAIRES – SAMPLE RESULT

Question 25. Providing a vision for the team

Respondent 1	Respondent 2	Respondent 3	Respondent 4	Respondent 5	Respondent 6	Your average for this question	Average for managers in this organisation	Your assessment of yourself
4	3	1	2	5	3	3	3.2	4

IDENTIFYING COMPETENCY GAPS

ATTITUDE SURVEYS

Attitude or climate surveys are excellent tools for establishing how well-equipped and motivated people are to deliver expected performance. This is because such surveys give feedback not only about how the employees perceive the organisation, but also about what they think and believe.

So, with a well-designed survey, you can measure how much **knowledge** people (and exactly *which* people) have about the organisation and its goals; what **skills** certain groups of people are perceived to have and whether employee **attitudes** and **values** are in line with those outlined in the mission statement.

And of course, these surveys can be conducted **before training** to pinpoint the needs, and **after training** to measure its impact.

IDENTIFYING COMPETENCY GAPS

ATTITUDE SURVEYS – SAMPLE 1

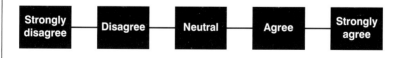

12. I have confidence in the management team of this organisation (please circle your answer).

Strongly disagree — **Disagree** — **Neutral** — **Agree** — **Strongly agree**

IDENTIFYING COMPETENCY GAPS
ATTITUDE SURVEYS – SAMPLE 2

32. Please describe what it's like to work in this organisation in terms of your own day-to-day experience.

....

....

....

....

....

....

....

TOOL BOX

IDENTIFYING COMPETENCY GAPS

OBSERVATION

Observation is the most 'hands-on' way to satisfy yourself regarding the learning needs of your potential course participants. There are two main approaches to observation:

Overt

This is where the individual knows they are being observed as they carry out a certain task. This approach has the advantage of openness and honesty. However it can sometimes alter the true level of performance because of issues unrelated to training (eg fear of management, trying to impress, or simply being in the spotlight, like in the famous Hawthorne experiments).

Covert

This is where you observe someone but don't let them know they're being watched or listened to. This has the advantage of giving you a view of uninhibited performance, but is morally questionable in most cases. Exceptions could include jobs where public safety is involved or other critical jobs where incumbents agree to unannounced spot checks on their behaviour. For example, 'help-desk' employees who accept that any of their phone calls with customers could be recorded 'for quality purposes'.

IDENTIFYING COMPETENCY GAPS

STAKEHOLDER ANALYSIS

Stakeholders are individuals and groups who have an interest in the performance of the target group for your training.

- Everyone has a **customer** for the work they do, even if that customer is someone internal in the organisation

- Everybody has **people who depend upon them** for product, services or support

Often, these stakeholders can be a rich and speedy source of information to back up and verify some of your assumptions about learning needs. The question you will specifically be asking the stakeholders is:

'What do you think these people need in terms of knowledge, skills and attitudes that will help them to meet the new performance goals?'

IDENTIFYING COMPETENCY GAPS

STAKEHOLDER ANALYSIS – WHO TO ASK?

- These stakeholders can be contacted personally or by email to save time
- Some of their views will be more important than others so you will need to weight and prioritise your inputs

TOOL BOX

IDENTIFYING COMPETENCY GAPS
KNOWLEDGE PRE-TESTS

The best way to find out if someone knows something is to ask them! Tests can be conducted at the beginning of a course to establish the gap in participants' knowledge of what you're going to teach them or, better still, before they actually come on the course so that you only train those who need the training. Example of a knowledge pre-test:

MOTIVATION THEORY TEST

1. Maslow described: Four ❑   Two ❑   Six ❑

    levels of motivation *(please check one)*

2. Adam's Equity Theory deals with expectancy   TRUE   FALSE

    (Please circle one)

IDENTIFYING COMPETENCY GAPS

PERFORMANCE APPRAISAL – DEFINITION

A regular (usually annual) review of a person's performance against targets and standards, carried out by their boss, who first completes an appraisal form (see page 74) and then holds a structured two-way interview with the person. In many organisations these days the annual appraisal interview includes an 'upward' appraisal where the employees also rates and gives feedback to the boss.

A well-designed and well-conducted appraisal system is the simplest and most cost-effective way of identifying competency gaps, as long as there is clarity about:

- The job to be done
- The progress that is being made
- The competencies required to meet new performance goals
- The 'dose' of competence required to fill the gaps between present and desired performance in the new goal areas
- The type of knowledge, skills and/or attitude training that could help fill those gaps

TOOL BOX

IDENTIFYING COMPETENCY GAPS
PERFORMANCE APPRAISAL – COMPONENTS

To conduct a performance appraisal effectively you need:

- **A job profile** form to give clarity about the role of the person being appraised (see next page)

- **Interim appraisal notes** – notes made on performance issues and incidents discussed at quarterly appraisal meetings to ensure fair and unbiased coverage of annual performance when the time comes

- **Annual appraisal form** – a template for conducting the annual appraisal session with each team member

IDENTIFYING COMPETENCY GAPS
PERFORMANCE APPRAISAL – JOB PROFILE

A typical job profile form looks something like this:

Name of job ....

Purpose of job ....

Short-term goals ....

Long-term goals ....

Key result areas ....

Key tasks ....

Competencies needed to perform tasks satisfactorily

....

TOOL BOX

IDENTIFYING COMPETENCY GAPS
PERFORMANCE APPRAISAL – ANNUAL APPRAISAL FORM

A typical appraisal form contains:

- Admin details
- Job objectives and results achieved
- Standards of performance for on-going tasks and performance achieved
- Descriptions of competencies needed to perform tasks satisfactorily and rating on each one
- Space for job holder's comments on ratings
- Learning and development needs and plans to meet them
- Actions agreed

FOCUS GROUPS

Focus groups are just what they sound like – groups of people who come together to focus on an issue with a view to resolving a problem or deciding something. They usually get together in short-burst meetings of up to 90 minutes which are facilitated using an agreed format.

As far as LNA is concerned, focus groups could be used for:

- Identifying competencies that a group of employees need to develop in order to meet new performance goals

- Brainstorming the many ways particular competencies can be developed/ strengthened

FOCUS GROUPS
FACILITATING FOCUS GROUPS

1. Start with a 'focus' question to inspire interest and/or identify how much people know/don't know about the topic. You can represent this on a flipchart and ask members to step forward and place a mark at the level that corresponds to their position on the issue.

2. Ask a 'discussion' question such as, *'What are the competencies we need to develop in communication?'* or, *'How can we develop the competency, "communicates well with customers"?'*

3. Ask members to write ideas on separate cards so that you can cluster them on a board.

4. Create actionable items from card clusters.

TOOL BOX

WRITING LEARNING OBJECTIVES

The best way to write learning objectives is to think of the acronym **SAS**.

SITUATION   What situation will the learner be in when they are demonstrating that they can do this task skillfully?

ACTION   What specifically will they be able to do when the training session is over?

STANDARD   Some measure by which we will be able to judge success

WRITING LEARNING OBJECTIVES

EXAMPLE

By the end of this training session:

SITUATION   Given a calculator and the day's takings.....

ACTION   participants will be able to balance the cash book.....

STANDARD   to 100% accuracy

TOOL BOX

THE LEARNING TRANSFER BRIDGE (8Ps)

There's no point in doing LNA unless what gets trained gets transferred – transferred back to the workplace in the form of improved performance. Although you, as the training professional, can't be held fully responsible for designing and managing the transfer process, you can influence its success. Here are eight things that need to be in place as a 'bridge' back to the participant's job to help make training work. We call them the 8Ps:

1. **Performance Improvement Plan** for each individual in the organisation.
2. **Participation of line management** in the design and delivery of training.
3. **Pre-course briefings** between participants and their bosses.
4. **Preparation of learning logs** to chart individuals' progress in learning.
5. **Programme support** before, during and after the training.
6. **Post-course briefing** between participants and their bosses.
7. **Peer and team support** after training.
8. **Prizes and sanctions** to reward new behaviour and sanction lack of it.

TOOL BOX

THE LEARNING TRANSFER BRIDGE (8Ps)

 1. PERFORMANCE IMPROVEMENT PLAN

Human performance improvement starts with a plan. As trainers we are responsible, along with line management, for making sure that every individual has an opportunity at least once a year to talk to their manager about how to do things better – *how to* means being given new performance targets. The results of this discussion, whether it takes place as part of the annual appraisal or at a separate meeting, should be recorded on the Performance Improvement Plan (PIP). Keep the PIP simple but include the following:

- **LINK** How does this person's performance link with and contribute to the overall performance of the organisation?

- **GAP** What is the gap between the person's present performance and the standards, objectives, new performance goals for the job. How was the gap measured? (See Identifying Competency Gaps on pages 58-74)

THE LEARNING TRANSFER BRIDGE (8Ps)

1. PERFORMANCE IMPROVEMENT PLAN

- **SOLUTIONS** What training does the person need to help bring about improved performance? What other development activities should be planned (job rotation, secondment, promotion, etc)? What other non-training actions might help (salary increase, job enrichment, process changes, etc)?

- **RESOURCES NEEDED** What are the costs of these actions in terms of money, equipment, staffing, etc?

- **OBSTACLES** Be realistic! What things will be hindering the achievement of the plan (environment, culture, motivation of others, etc)?

- **MEASUREMENT** Finally, how will improvement be measured and rewarded (objectives, follow-up, etc)?

THE LEARNING TRANSFER BRIDGE (8Ps)

 ## 2. PARTICIPATION OF LINE MANAGEMENT

Line managers' inputs are vital when we start to create training solutions for filling performance gaps. Here are some guidelines:

- Get managers to sign-off on the learning objectives which you will use to design the learning events

- Note down how the learning process in the courses you are designing will deliver what managers expect

THE LEARNING TRANSFER BRIDGE (8Ps)

2. PARTICIPATION OF LINE MANAGEMENT

- Train managers to contribute at least one module to each course. OK, so they're not very professional trainers, but you can limit a potential 'delivery disaster' by providing your exercises, or by 'topping and tailing' the sessions with your own input. Even if managers are not as good as you are at giving punchy training messages, the results will at least be linked to what they really want and need – and therefore they will know what behaviours they will measure and reward back on the job.

- If this is not realistic in terms of managers' skills and/or availability, ask them (cajole, coax, blackmail!) at least to open and close training events. This will lend credibility and impact to the training, as will impromptu, interested visits by managers to training courses. Apart from anything else, this involvement keeps managers in tune with what training is trying to do to help **them** help their people to improve.

THE LEARNING TRANSFER BRIDGE (8Ps)

3. PRE-COURSE BRIEFINGS

This is one of the most valuable steps in making sure that learning is transferred into performance improvement. Honestly speaking, how many participants on your training courses have had serious, job-related briefing sessions with their bosses before they come? How many have discussed their mutual expectations as to what they will learn and how they will put it into practice back on the job?

Your role as a trainer is to make sure these briefings take place. It's the old story, isn't it? Unless someone knows what is expected of them how will they know whether they've achieved anything?

TOOL BOX

THE LEARNING TRANSFER BRIDGE (8Ps)

3. PRE-COURSE BRIEFINGS

One of the best ways to conduct a pre-course briefing is to use the PIP (Performance Improvement Plan) or to refer back to the most recent appraisal discussion and to define some key learning objectives for the course. You can help managers to set clear, behaviourally stated targets and insist that they agree on a date for a post-course briefing (see page 90).

Here are some examples of typical objectives formulated at a pre-course briefing.

At the end of this course the trainee will:

- Be able to use the new XYZ software
- Have learned and practised new presentation techniques
- Have acquired the knowledge about new EU regulations in order to modify ABC
- Be able to explain the new mission and values statement to the team
- Know and have practised the steps involved in a good selection interview

Maybe you should insist upon signed evidence that a pre-course briefing has taken place before you allow anyone to attend a course! Sometimes, by making something more difficult to have, you make it more desirable.

THE LEARNING TRANSFER BRIDGE (8Ps)

4. PREPARATION OF LEARNING LOGS

In order to allow people to track their progress as they acquire new knowledge, skills and attitudes, many organisations have introduced individual **learning logs**. These logs provide people with an on-going record of their learning achievements and of the steps they are taking/still need to take on the journey to improved performance.

There's an example of what could be covered in such a document on the next page.

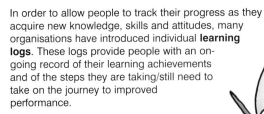

TOOL BOX

COURSE LEARNING LOG

1. **Expectations** – what am I expected to achieve/do before, during and after the course?

2. **Manager's role** – how will s/he provide support?

3. **Trainer's role** – how can the trainer help me most?

4. **My learning objectives** – based on the course learning objectives. How to measure?

5. **Notes from pre-course briefing** – details of discussion with my boss.

6. **Course notes** – notes on learning, spot evaluations of relevance, satisfaction, etc.

7. **Learning achievements** – what did I actually learn? How can I prove it?

8. **Action plans from post-course briefing** – performance objectives set during post-course briefing.

9. **Obstacles** – things/people/environmental issues, etc that could be working against achieving these objectives.

10. **Plans to overcome these obstacles** – how can my boss/colleagues help me?

THE LEARNING TRANSFER BRIDGE (8Ps)

5. PROGRAMME SUPPORT

There is no doubt that current training lowers current productivity. People can't attend a course **and** do their jobs at 100% efficiency. Nor should they be expected to get back to 100% immediately after a course. They should have some time to practise the new learning.

This is not easy because it often means a change of attitude from both the manager and the trainee. In some cases it also means a change in the culture of the organisation from 'training as a perk' to 'training as a vital investment for growth'.

THE LEARNING TRANSFER BRIDGE (8Ps)

5. PROGRAMME SUPPORT

Before a course As a trainer, you should be coaching managers on how to create an environment where people like learning. Managers could start by setting a good example – by being learning individuals themselves. Just as with learning organisations, managers need to encourage learning every day, in meetings, discussions, appraisals. They can do this by asking questions, reviewing PIPs regularly, commenting on their own learning, etc. On the practical side, both the manager and the trainee should be planning **how to cover the trainee's job** during the learning to avoid stress and worry.

During a course Above all, the boss should **leave the trainee in peace** during the training! No phone calls for information. No frantic emails. On the contrary, maybe a note or call of encouragement during the course, or, even better, a lightning visit to the training venue for a chat on how it's going.

After a course Because most people these days are overloaded with work, they often have to put off practising new skills and techniques until that magic day when they will suddenly have enough time. Managers and trainers need to recognise that the implementation of learning will require that some tasks be reallocated, or quite simply postponed, so that the trainee can concentrate on trying out the new skills.

THE LEARNING TRANSFER BRIDGE (8Ps)

6. POST-COURSE BRIEFINGS

All the research data on the transfer of learning says, *'The longer you wait, the less you will use it'*. So, the first few days following any learning event are a vital time.
As soon as possible after the course, the trainee and their boss should sit down and talk about how to put the new knowledge, skills and/or attitudes into practice – basing their discussion on the pre-course briefing (see pages 84-85).

Specifically this will mean:

- Turning pre-course learning objectives into performance objectives

- Identifying obstacles to achieving these objectives and starting to plan how to overcome them. Don't forget that many of these plans may involve peer and team support (see pages 92-93)

.....and noting everything on the trainee's learning log!

TOOL BOX

THE LEARNING TRANSFER BRIDGE (8Ps)

 ## 6. POST-COURSE BRIEFINGS

Examples of learning objectives (see page 85) turned into performance objectives following a course:

1. All my sales reports will be produced on XYZ software by the year end.
2. My next three presentations will have been structured using the newly learned model, and the feedback sheet I distribute will show a score of over three out of five for 'body language'.
3. By July 31st we'll have rewritten our ABC procedures in line with new EU legislation.
4. I will have conducted two 'mission and values' meetings with my team before the end of September and obtained an 80% commitment to the statement.
5. By October 31st, an observer will have confirmed that at least two selection interviews I conducted followed the steps learned.

Examples of obstacles to achieving objectives two and four:

- Time/opportunity to practise (objective two)
- Acceptability of feedback sheet to audience (objective two)
- Acceptability to team members of 'being told values' (objective four)

THE LEARNING TRANSFER BRIDGE (8Ps)

7. PEER AND TEAM SUPPORT

As we saw in the post-course briefing session (previous page), trainees' bosses will have worked with them to set objectives for putting training into practice in the workplace and will have helped to identify obstacles to doing this.

In order to help overcome these obstacles (noted on the trainee's learning log) the boss will have to take a team approach. One approach is to organise **sharing sessions** when a team member returns from a training course. The trainee presents the key learning points to his/her colleagues and discusses the relevance of this learning to the job. The learning log can then be used to jot down **agreements on the support which each colleague will provide**.

THE LEARNING TRANSFER BRIDGE (8Ps)

7. PEER AND TEAM SUPPORT

Because the trainee will need time and space to practise, the manager should help to restructure his/her workload. As mentioned on page 89 under Programme Support, this may mean temporarily allocating certain of the trainee's tasks to other team members (whether or not they volunteer!).

The manager might also provide support by establishing learning pairs within the team. A learning pair is simply two team members who have attended the same training event, and whose job is to compare notes on the effectiveness of the training received and to support each other as they try to put the learning to work.

THE LEARNING TRANSFER BRIDGE (8Ps)

8. PRIZES AND SANCTIONS

It's sad but true that, most of the time, in most organisations, most people are not specifically rewarded for putting into practice what they learned in training. On the contrary, they're sometimes actually **punished** for trying to!

- *'Enjoyed the holiday? Now back to the real world'*

- *'Don't rock the boat now, just because you've been on a fancy training programme'*

- *'We're not having any of that 'touchy-feely' stuff in this department, I can tell you!'*

- *'We'd love to use these new systems but we simply can't afford the equipment needed'*

TOOL BOX

THE LEARNING TRANSFER BRIDGE (8Ps)

8. PRIZES AND SANCTIONS

Just imagine how much more seriously training would be taken if people's salaries (or even just their bonuses) were dependent on them putting into practice what they learned on courses!

Without going that far, prizes for new behaviours come in many forms:

- Salary increases
- Bonus payments
- Praise and recognition
- New and more interesting projects
- Higher quality of working life

And, as a last thought, how could you 'sanction' people for not doing what they learned in training? That's where your motivational creativity comes in!

EVALUATION

THE FOUR LEVELS

In 1959, Donald Kirkpatrick published a series of articles on training evaluation in the journal of the American Society for Training and Development (now known as ASTD). The four levels of evaluation were born.

Since then they have stood the test of time and, although they have been 'tweaked' and added to over the years, they remain the basic tool for trainers to assess whether their training is effective. The four levels are summarised on the next page. For more details on training evaluation please refer to *The Training Evaluation Pocketbook*.

TOOL BOX

EVALUATION

THE FOUR LEVELS

- **REACTION** Did the participants like the course? The famous 'happy sheet'. Get all participants to complete one at the end of each course

- **LEARNING** Did the participants learn anything? Test their knowledge, skills and/or attitudes toward the topic at the end of the training. If you want to be sure that the training caused the learning you have to test them at the beginning too!

- **BEHAVIOUR** Did the participants change their behaviour as a result of the training? Test the behaviour after the training: probably three to six months later to allow the changes to kick in

- **RESULTS** Were the organisation's results affected positively by the training, as per the CEO's expectations from your training needs investigation?

FURTHER BROWSING

All that's left to do now is to complete and score the questionnaire in our last chapter and set out on the road to a realistic and results-oriented Learning Needs Analysis within your organisation. To help you on your way and to keep the tank topped up as you travel, here are some key websites that will allow you to keep up with the developments in LNA:

Chartered Institute of Personnel and Development:
www.cipd.co.uk

Irish Institute of Training & Development:
www.iitd.ie

Society for Organizational Learning:
www.solonline.org/?home

Association for Talent Development:
www.astd.org

Skills –Third Sector:
www.skillsthirdsector.org.uk/training_needs_analysis/resources_websites

QUESTIONNAIRE

How easy will it be to make LNA
work for you?

EXPLANATION OF QUESTIONNAIRE

This questionnaire comprises 30 questions for you to ask of your organisation. The questions concern human resource systems and techniques which help to smooth the way for a good training needs analysis.

For each question you simply answer 'Yes', 'No' or 'Not Applicable'.

On page 108 you'll find out how to score and what your scores mean in terms of how easy it's going to be to make LNA work for you.

QUESTIONNAIRE

STANDARDS OF PERFORMANCE

		Yes	No	N/A
1.	Are organisational performance standards clear (eg production targets, quality requirements, etc)?			
2.	Are objectives set for all staff and related to organisational targets?			
3.	Are performance standards set for each job?			
4.	Have core competencies been defined for the organisation?			
5.	Have core competencies been defined for specific jobs?			
6.	Are long-term training needs identified at a strategic level, linked to long-term goals?			

QUESTIONNAIRE

MEASUREMENT SYSTEM

	Yes	No	N/A
7. Is the organisation's performance measured (eg production targets, quality requirements, etc)?			
8. Do shortfalls in organisational performance get analysed for training requirements?			
9. Is each individual's performance in meeting their objectives measured?			
10. Are people monitored for their achievement of on-going performance standards?			
11. Are people measured against the core competencies for their role?			
12. Are people's shortfalls in performance analysed for training needs?			

QUESTIONNAIRE

MANAGER'S ROLE

	Yes	No	N/A
13. Do managers regularly communicate business plans, strategies, goals to their team?			
14. Are managers held accountable for the development of their staff?			
15. Is informal coaching part of the culture of the organisation?			
16. Is an appraisal system in place in the organisation?			
17. Do people get regular and accurate feedback from managers about their performance?			
18. Does the appraisal system generate personal development plans for everyone?			

REWARD SYSTEM

	Yes	No	N/A
19. Is good performance rewarded?			
20. Is the reward system fair and consistent?			
21. Does the reward system include options like extra responsibility, career development opportunities, training, etc.?			

Well Done!

CAREER PLANNING AND DEVELOPMENT

	Yes	No	N/A
22. Are individual's career aspirations understood and planned for?			
23. Do people get feedback on career development issues?			
24. Are training needs for career development identified and addressed?			

QUESTIONNAIRE

SUCCESSION PLANNING

	Yes	No	N/A
25. Are future job demands for the organisation understood?			
26. Is there an up-to-date succession plan for the organisation/ departments?			
27. Are managers held responsible for training and developing their people for succession purposes?			

RECRUITMENT AND SELECTION

	Yes	No	N/A
28. Is there a consistent and robust recruitment and selection process in place?			
29. Are candidates' skill/competency levels matched to job demands when recruiting?			
30. Is there a well-designed and useful induction programme?			

QUESTIONNAIRE

SCORING

How easy will it be for you to make LNA work in your organisation? Well, the better the human resource systems in place, the easier it will be for you to establish training needs and provide **sustainable** solutions.

Please count the number of 'Yes' answers you've given on the questionnaire.

25-30 Great chances of a smooth ride!

15-25 You may have to work on improving some HR systems before hoping for total success.

10-15 Lack of underpinning from HR systems could make it tough to get enough good data from your learning needs analysis.

0-10 An uphill struggle could be looming – unless you are also the HR Manager and are in a start-up phase!

About the Authors

Paul Donovan, MSc, Mgmt. MSc T&L, D.Soc.Sci.
Paul Donovan is School Director of Teaching and Learning at
the school of Business and Law, NUI, Maynooth. He was
previously Registrar and Head of Management at Irish
Management Institute (IMI) specialising in Management
Development. Before joining IMI he worked as a general
operations manager with the Bord na Mona, the Irish Peat
Development Authority. He was also training and development
manager of Bord na Mona group.

Paul has delivered executive development programmes in over 15 countries.
He has written several peer reviewed articles, over 10 books in training and general
management. He has contributed a column to HRD magazine for over 13 years.
His research interest is the transfer of training. Paul holds two masters degrees from
Trinity College Dublin and a doctorate from Leicester University.

About the Authors

John Townsend, BA MA MCIPD
John has built a reputation internationally as a leading trainer of trainers. He is founder of the highly-regarded Master Trainer Institute, a total learning facility located just outside Geneva which draws trainers and facilitators from around the world. He set up the Institute after 30 years' experience in international consulting and human resources management positions in the UK, France, the United States and Switzerland – notably as a European Director of Executive development with GTE in Geneva where he had training responsibility for over 800 managers in 15 countries.

During his long career as a trainer of trainers he has not only helped to spread the unique Master Trainer Institute philosophy across the world via his conferences, seminars and bestselling training videos, but also written a number of widely translated management and professional guides.

Pocketbooks – *available in both paperback and digital formats*

360 Degree Feedback*
Absence Management
Appraisals
Assertiveness
Balance Sheet
Body Language
Business Planning
Career Transition
Coaching
Cognitive Behavioural Coaching
Communicator's
Competencies
Confidence
Creative Manager's
C.R.M.
Cross-cultural Business
Customer Service
Decision-making
Delegation
Developing People
Discipline & Grievance
Diversity*
Emotional Intelligence
Empowerment*
Energy and Well-being
Facilitator's
Feedback
Flexible Working*
Handling Complaints

Handling Resistance
Icebreakers
Impact & Presence
Improving Efficiency
Improving Profitability
Induction
Influencing
Interviewer's
I.T. Trainer's
Key Account Manager's
Leadership
Learner's
Management Models
Manager's
Managing Assessment Centres
Managing Budgets
Managing Cashflow
Managing Change
Managing Customer Service
Managing Difficult Participants
Managing Recruitment
Managing Upwards
Managing Your Appraisal
Marketing
Mediation
Meetings
Memory
Mentoring
Motivation

Negotiator's
Networking
NLP
Nurturing Innovation
Openers & Closers
People Manager's
Performance Management
Personal Success
Positive Mental Attitude
Presentations
Problem Behaviour
Project Management
Psychometric Testing
Resolving Conflict
Reward*
Sales Excellence
Salesperson's*
Self-managed Development
Starting In Management
Storytelling
Strategy
Stress
Succeeding at Interviews
Sustainability
Tackling Difficult Conversations
Talent Management
Teambuilding Activities
Teamworking
Telephone Skills

Thinker's
Time Management
Trainer's
Training Evaluation
Training Needs Analysis
Transfer of Learning
Transformative Change
Virtual Teams
Vocal Skills
Working Relationships
Workplace Politics
Writing Skills

only available as an e-book

Pocketfiles

Trainer's Blue Pocketfile of
Ready-to-use Activities

Trainer's Green Pocketfile of
Ready-to-use Activities

Trainer's Red Pocketfile of
Ready-to-use Activities

To order please visit us at **www.pocketbook.co.uk**

23.09.14

ORDER FORM

No.
copies

Your details

Name _____

Position _____

Company _____

Address _____

_____

_____

Telephone _____

Fax _____

E-mail _____

VAT No. (EC companies) _____

Your Order Ref _____

Please send me:

The _Learning Needs Analysis_ Pocketbook [ ]

The _____ Pocketbook [ ]

The _____ Pocketbook [ ]

The _____ Pocketbook [ ]

Order by Post
MANAGEMENT POCKETBOOKS LTD
LAUREL HOUSE, STATION APPROACH,
ALRESFORD, HAMPSHIRE SO24 9JH UK

Order by Phone, Fax or Internet
Telephone: +44 (0)1962 735573
Facsimile: +44 (0)1962 733637
E-mail: sales@pocketbook.co.uk
Web: www.pocketbook.co.uk

Customers in USA should contact:
Management Pocketbooks
2427 Bond Street, University Park, IL 60466
Telephone: 866 620 6944   Facsimile: 708 534 7803
E-mail: mp.orders@ware-pak.com
Web: www.managementpocketbooks.com